Hay que cuidar el bosque

por Rita Crosby

Scott Foresman
is an imprint of

PEARSON

Glenview, Illinois • Boston, Massachusetts • Chandler, Arizona
Upper Saddle River, New Jersey

Every effort has been made to secure permission and provide appropriate credit for photographic material. The publisher deeply regrets any omission and pledges to correct errors called to its attention in subsequent editions.

Unless otherwise acknowledged, all photographs are the property of Pearson.

Photo locations denoted as follows: Top (T), Center (C), Bottom (B), Left (L), Right (R), Background (Bkgd)

Opener (C) Digital Vision, Opener (Bkgd) Digital Vision; 1 (C) Digital Vision; 3 (C) Digital Vision, 3 (T) Getty Images, 3 (BL) Brand X Pictures; 4 (TL) © Dorling Kindersley, 4 (C) Digital Vision; 5 (C) © Comstock Inc., 5 (BR) Brand X Pictures; 6 (C) ©Max Whittaker/Reuters/Landov LLC, 6 (BR) ©David McNew/Getty Images; 7 (C) ©David R. Frazier Photolibrary, Inc./Alamy, 7 (TL) ©Nigel Bean/Nature Picture Library; 8 (C) Digital Vision, 8 (BL) ImageState

ISBN 13: 978-0-328-53310-7
ISBN 10:   0-328-53310-6

Copyright © by Pearson Education, Inc., or its affiliates. All rights reserved. Printed in the United States of America. This publication is protected by copyright, and permission should be obtained from the publisher prior to any prohibited reproduction, storage in a retrieval system, or transmission in any form or by any means, electronic, mechanical, photocopying, recording, or likewise. For information regarding permissions, write to Pearson Curriculum Rights & Permissions, One Lake Street, Upper Saddle River, New Jersey 07458.

Pearson® is a trademark, in the U.S. and/or other countries, of Pearson plc or its affiliates.

Scott Foresman® is a trademark, in the U.S. and/or other countries, of Pearson Education, Inc., or its affiliates.

2 3 4 5 6 7 8 9 10 V0N4 13 12 11 10

Este bosque es un buen lugar para los pájaros y otros animales.

Aquí viven y encuentran comida.

Este bosque es un buen lugar para las flores y los árboles.

Aquí obtienen agua y luz del sol para vivir.

Este bosque es un buen lugar para divertirse.

Estos niños miran las hojas que caen de los árboles.

Miran los pájaros y otros animales.

Reman botes en el lago.

Estos trabajadores cuidan los bosques.

Combaten y apagan los incendios.

Cortan los árboles enfermos.

Luego plantan árboles nuevos.

Así estos animales no pierden su hogar.

Así pueden encontrar comida.

Todos debemos cuidar el bosque.

El bosque es un buen hogar para los árboles, los pájaros y otros animales.

¿Qué vas a hacer tú para cuidar el bosque?